WHITE ROOMS

WHITE ROOMS

Jordi Sarrà

COLLINS | DESIGN

An Imprint of HarperCollinsPublishers

WHITE ROOMS

HarperCollins books may be purchased for educational, business, or sales promotional use.
For information, please write: Special Markets Department, HarperCollins *Publishers* Inc.,
10 East 53rd Street, New York, NY 10022

First Edition published in 2006 by:
Collins Design
An Imprint of HarperCollins*Publishers*
10 East 53rd Street
New York, NY 10022
Tel.: (212) 207-7000
Fax: (212) 207-7654
CollinsDesign@harpercollins.com
www.harpercollins.com

Distributed throughout the world by:
HarperCollins*Publishers*
10 East 53rd Street
New York, NY 10022
Fax: (212) 207-7654

Packaged by
LOFT Publications
Via Laietana 32, 4.º Of. 92
08003 Barcelona, Spain
Tel.: +34 932 688 088
Fax: +34 932 687 073
loft@loftpublications.com
www.loftpublications.com

Editor:
Jordi Sarrà

Texts:
Eva Millet, Cristian Campos

Translator:
Jay Noden

Photographer:
Jordi Sarrà

Stylist:
Marta Feduchi

Art Director:
Mireia Casanovas Soley

Layout:
Ignasi Gracia Blanco

Collaborators:
Estela Gómez Lupión (stylist), Allan James Stuart (stylist), and Montse Garriga (photographer)

Library of Congress Cataloging-in-Publication Data

Millet, Eva.
  White rooms / Eva Millet.– 1st ed.
    p. cm.
  ISBN-13: 978-0-06-082992-6 (hardcover)
  ISBN-10: 0-06-082992-3 (hardcover)
  1. White in interior decoration. I. Millet, Eva. II. Title.
  NK2115.5.C6S277 2006
  747'.94--dc22
                          2006002078

Printed by: Anman Gràfiques del Vallès, Spain

First Printing, 2006

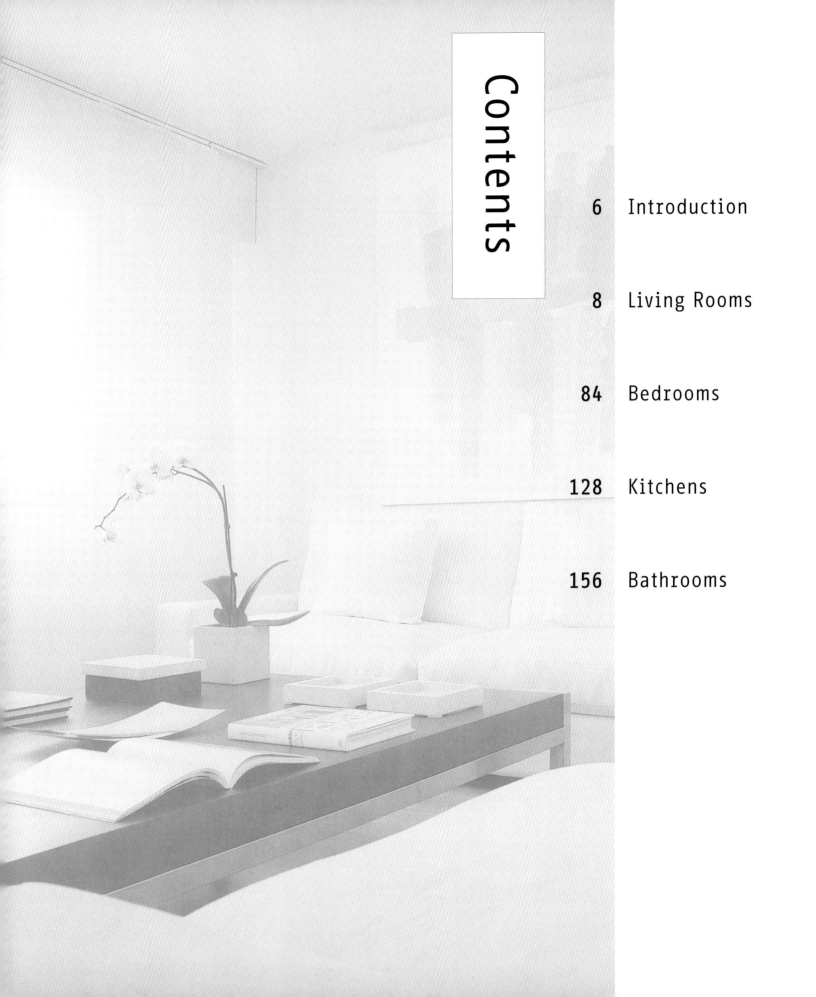

Contents

The generous color

Despite its discretion, white is the most generous color that exists. It has the power to accentuate spaces and other tones of the spectrum. These three virtues have transformed it into a resource that has been widely used, both in architecture and interior design, throughout history. Mediterranean houses have been whitewashed from top to bottom for centuries, and cold and glamorous marble floors date back to the Roman era. The wooden floors and ceilings of Northern Europe are still painted in subtle shades of broken white, while the refined shapes of rationalist buildings identify themselves by this color.

Synonymous with modernism and minimalism, white has been used for decades as another architectural resource: white walls, for example, enlarge the space and accentuate any object and shape attached to them. White also has an important presence in the everyday objects that decorate our houses: in a set of crisp cotton sheets or in a pile of soft, fluffy towels; in the transparency of curtains that filter the light; in the discreet shine of a porcelain cup; or in the serene presence of a paint-stripped piece of furniture.

White is always a safe bet. As it never goes out of fashion, and maybe because it is the sum of all the colors of the spectrum, it has many shades and a certain aura of mystery. They say that in the language of Eskimos there are dozens of words to describe snow and its different tones. In ours there are also plenty of words to describe the shades of white: snow white, ice, ivory, broken, porcelain, chalk, foam, grey, milky, mushroom, pearl, silver, magnolia, gardenia…

White exudes serenity: there is nothing more relaxing than a white room flooded by light. In many cultures around the world white is associated with purity, tranquility, balance, holiness, and goodness. It can be the color for brides or for mourning, and is a sign of peace recognized throughout the world. Its possibilities are endless and its use rarely appears excessive. The pages of this book, featuring interiors where white plays the leading role, are good examples of this and the best test amount to the fact that this classic color, far from being boring, has an infinite capacity to create unique atmospheres.

Living Rooms

Art galleries often have white walls to highlight the pieces being exhibited; paradoxically, their neutrality lends strength to any object or tone attached to them. In the living room, traditionally the most dignified room of any home as well as a place of rest and for socializing, we can often find furniture, paintings, souvenirs, and details with aesthetic or sentimental value. This is why choosing white, whether it is on the walls, the upholstery, the furniture, or the flooring, will always be a sure bet. Also, white does not distract one's view, and when applied will therefore highlight the architecture of the room. Since the middle of the nineteenth century, when Charles Rennie Mackintosh caused a sensation by decorating the living room of his home in Glasgow in white including the walls, floors, and a large part of the furniture, this colour has become commonplace in living rooms, whether it is monochromatic or combined with wooden surfaces, vivid colours, metals, or glass.

Left: Some of the furniture (the sofa, the round lamp, the vase on top of the pile of books, and the potted cactus) transposes the white of the walls to the center of the room. The round red rug, situated in the center of the room, adds a touch of color, lending elegance to the whole effect.

Above: In interior design, white acts as a great decorative canvas on which to embellish other tones, textures, and forms, regardless of their size. This is what is happening with the application in this image, whose base, a branch of red coral, stands out dramatically on the white background.

11

Above: Natural light has the power to fracture white into an amalgam of shades. Filtered by cotton curtains and reflected on the wall, the light that shines through creates diverse shades of white on the left-hand wall.

Right: A white bookshelf in front of a white wall illuminated by natural light creates an optical effect whereby the objects placed on it seem to float in midair. The brightly colored furniture and objects in the rooms become the focal point of the space.

Left: Some spaces receive an excess of natural light, which can be overly reflected on white walls and floors. However, this effect can be mitigated by installing some frosted windows.

Above: Providing a white environment is the best way to make an especially prized piece of furniture or a painting stand out. A bunch of flowers on a white background guarantees an aesthetic impact.

Strong tones, such as the orange and the dark brown of this tropical wood flooring, appear toned down when contrasted with white, which is also recognized for its properties as a balancing tone, countering the strength of the other colors.

In this case, it is clear that surrounding certain decorative elements (the painting on the back wall and the orange armchair) by other white objects enhances the former, while the latter blend into the space and acquire a more subtle personality.

Left: The use of creams, beiges, and whites began to regain value in interior design toward the end of the eighties, and became a classic in the nineties, a decade that saw a growth of an interest in conservation, restoration, and a more natural lifestyle.

Above: The lamps with white shades project a powerful and diaphanous light. The use of any other color would fail to produce such a luminous effect within this austere space.

Left: Venetian blinds are recommended for spaces with straight lines and minimalist settings, but they can be rather impersonal and stark at times. This can be offset by some kind of decorative element with great character, like the two baroque-inspired photo frames.

Above: White has the power to lighten any structure, however thick or heavy it may be. This is the case with this bookcase, which blends with the white wall behind it without losing its practical function.

White is a powerful color that changes in different light, and can affect surrounding colors by maximizing their intensity.

Here, the total predominance of white has been broken by a compelling and colorful decorative element: the red and blue painting on the back wall. The sofa and the low lacquered table have been converted into the nerve center of the space.

Above: Although it can appear monotonous, white has dozens of tones: from snow white to milky white; broken, dirty, to cream whites; or magnolia and gardenia whites that are widely used in Anglo-Saxon countries to paint walls and façades.

Right: A good way to introduce a subtle contrast is by working with different materials and textures: from the hexagonal floor tiles to the plastic of the round table in the center, to the texture of the curtains and the upholstery of the sofa.

Left: In interior design, white is the color *par excellence*. It will not be difficult to find decorative elements and accessories in this color, from a simple ashtray to the lampshade, to a chair and hundreds of different cushions.

Above: White flowers (including irises, roses, tulips, camellias and daffodils) also have many shades. Some are tinted by a pale green, others by yellow, cream, or pink.

Above: For some, white is anything but a neutral tone; a white space possesses many shades and is the perfect base for any object, even when the object is also white.

Right: In this case, the purity of white enhances and gives strength to the purity of shapes of the furniture in this austere and rather spartan dining room. The result is risky yet aesthetically coherent choice.

The great architects have worked with white, applying it as much in their structures as in the furniture. This is the case with Mies van der Rohe, whose name is synonymous with rationalism, and who designed the famous Barcelona armchair, which we see here upholstered in white leather.

The Barcelona chair takes pride of place in this room. The painting on the back wall is the only object able to compete and deprive it of a certain prominence. To choose a painting other than a white one would alter the effect and spoil the harmony of the whole composition.

Left: The reverse solution has been adopted: adorning the room with a sizeable white painting is not detrimental to the prominence of the wood-colored low table in the center. Both options are equally acceptable.

Above: The strength of white combined with black is especially reflected in photography, where the combination of both colors continues to be a classic. In the lounge on the right a part of the wall is covered with images in this format.

Above: As white is the color of light, so green is the color of nature. This is why both go splendidly alongside each other, becoming a decorative resource as simple as it is striking as can be.

Right: A silky, thin curtain diffuses the light and the outlines of the surrounding objects. A metal chest of drawers reflects the light and lends the space an even more ethereal air.

In this living room, the combination of porcelain white and soft beige creates a theatrical and dreamy effect.

The different shades of a color (cream can be seen as a shade of white) combine perfectly in most cases. White is not an exception, which explains the presence of these cream-colored sofas in a white setting.

The "star" artifacts, usually antique furniture or valuable works of art, are those around which the structure of the room is created. The photographs on these pages show two examples of living rooms laid out to display the valuable, eye-catching centerpieces to their best effect. The white surroundings consolidate their pride of place.

Above: The capacity to create atmospheres impregnated with a certain mystery is another one of the qualities resulting from the application of white and its many shades. A sliding door with an old-fashioned mirror emphasizes the enigmatic presence of this color.

Right: The intense red color has a dynamic quality that helps to balance an environment that might be deemed too static or relaxed. The blue of the painting finds its counterpoint in the small features, such as the candles on the table.

Above: A surprising range of whites exist, depending on the materials, textures, and light in a room. In this living room, the tone transmits an absolute serenity, and invites rest.

Right: White is the color *par excellence* of the dinner service and kitchen utensils; other colors may distract from the colors of the food and cause the food to seem unnatural.

Above: White is also the color of silence. It possesses a special mysticism and gives rise to relaxation and contemplation. The old refectories in monasteries were always in this tone to facilitate rest and introspection.

Right: Any decorative feature positioned on walls painted white really stands out. If this is also white, like the four paintings on the right, the feature, on the contrary, tends to be less obvious. The result is a calm elegance.

Left: The dinner service and kitchen decor are usually white because it symbolizes purity and hygiene. Thus the choice of white is based on purely an aesthetic criterion, and also on practicality: any stain will stand out more on a white background, so it will be easier to clean.

Above: The very French, paint-stripped furniture (surfaces from which the layer of paint has been removed) is more and more common in interior design. The technique provides unique tones of whites and grays, and can be placed in contemporary environments.

In art, white is an essential color. There are painters who have been obsessed with its purity and possibilities and have dedicated themselves exclusively to painting in this color. Others use it as a base to transform the smallest detail into the leading role. Neutral colored materials are without a doubt those most widely used by decorators and interior designers, given their capacity to combine perfectly with practically any other color. The only problem is that they do not easily harmonize with an excessive use of other colors. In the case of the photograph on the right, the maroon and black of the cushions are the only other colors used.

Sometimes, and especially if it is very intense, white merges with natural light to create a sensation of emptiness, of an unreal space without apparent limits.

A small space can be made larger either by removing walls or joining them, as is the case with this kitchen, dining room, and living room. Furthermore, painting the walls with a uniform color accentuates the effect of continuity and enhances the feeling o spaciousness.

White, together with black, is considered a "no color" because it does not compete with any other element of decoration. White allows for the creation of very different ambiences within a single dwelling, since it never demands prominence and is the perfect canvas on which to give expression to any idea.

Left: In this case, white has been reserved for the vertical elements (the wall, the table, and the staircase) while wood is the chosen material for the horizontal element (the small table, the surface of the individual steps and the low central table). The contrast works as long as this distinction is strictly maintained.

Above: White as a color for painting walls has been used since time immemorial. Whitewash (a mixture of water and dead lime without any added color), is not only hygienic but can also allow stone walls to breathe. The result is a floury surface that does not hide the texture of the surfaces.

61

Above: It looks as if it were a live painting, but this window frame painted in white accentuates the colors outside, both the green from the vegetation that covers the façade and the light blue of the sky.

Right: Two small skylights in this dwelling light up specific parts of the furniture, creating small boxes of light as though they were paintings hung on a flat surface. This characteristic should be converted into yet another decorative element.

White has been used as a decorative resource for many years, which is why there are so many antiques in this color, many of French or Scandinavian origin. In these Nordic countries white is the base of a famous decorative and Gustavian style.

White walls have the capacity to highlight beams, frames, and other architectural elements. A natural material such as wood, when combined with white, becomes another color. Sometimes it is a good idea to break with some of the seemingly immutable rules of interior design. A well-lit and spacious dwelling can seem even larger by having a minimum amount of furniture. The white color of the walls and ceiling further heightens the impression of limitless space.

Left: The owner of this dwelling has opted for the combination of different materials and textures in some decorative elements: the plant pots, the plastic-looking, shiny table, etc. All these elements do have a common denominator: their color belongs to the range of whites.

Above: The main disadvantage of white, its apparent lack of depth, is a factor that can be taken advantage of to give the light, colors, and materials in the room.

Above: Still lifes based on white are relaxed, since with the lack of shades competing against each other, allows the gaze to concentrate on areas of color (such as the yellow of the flowers), however few.

Right: An apparently discordant feature, such as the median high wall in the room, can be concealed or its predominance reduced by painting it white.

Left: The glass furniture, like this table, further accentuates the ethereal atmosphere of a room in which the walls, ceiling, and even the floor are. This excessively aseptic atmosphere can be improved by placing something with a strong presence on the glass table, such as the brown porcelain plate or the tortured willow twig here.

Above: Neutral tones have the ability to give strength to textures and natural materials, such as wood, clay, and even organic materials such as raffia, which particularly stand out on a white background.

In this living room a perfectly harmonized ambience has been achieved by following the ancient principles of "feng-shui," combining wood (table), fire (spotlights on the ceiling), earth (light yellow shades of the sofa), and metal (metallic doors separating the room from the exterior). The only element missing to complete the energy cycle is water.

Above: The discreet introduction of different shades of white can make a room a subtle palette of colors. This is the case in this lounge, decorated almost entirely in whites, where a light touch of beige has been introduced.

Right; It is advisable not to place decorative items in a straight line. It is better to superimpose them instead. Two different sized earthenware plates placed on a ledge behind the sofa are an elegant decorative idea.

Left: Leaving the walls bare of paintings or other decorative features focuses attention the floor pieces, the fireplace, and the pile of logs. It is an especially attractive option for large-sized rooms, where the decorative details need to be combined in a single space.

Above: Due to its capacity to fill a space and highlight forms, architects adore white, a color associated with modernity and minimalism, and which reflects ever-precious light like no other.

Fabrics are one of the most widely used resources in the decoration of interiors. In this case, beige checked upholstery gives color to a monochromatic room. This choice was possible thanks to the owner's decision to do without curtains. Otherwise the upholstery of the sofas would have to match the color of the curtains.

Bedrooms

The effect the use of shades of white produces in interior design is a feeling of space, tranquillity, and harmony. These three qualities are perfect for a bedroom, the room of the house that is traditionally a place of rest and intimacy. Four white walls guarantee rest for the eyes. A bedspread in this tone creates a sober and classic bed. Transparent curtains allow light to filter through seductively. A set of white sheets provide a safe and elegant choice, since they will never go out of fashion. There are infinite opportunities to play with white in the bedroom, positioning furniture, accessories, textiles, and even flowers, of this color. The decorative fittings and furniture are to be arranged around the bed—the centerpiece of the room. However, more can be done than simply choosing the color white as the only decorative element—the careful placement of the furniture around the room should maximize the available space and optimize the feeling of tranquillity and relaxation.

Above: White is the color that best highlights textures. From the bare wood of a child's seat to the transparency of a canopy of delicate cotton, surfaces of all kinds are embellished when painted or dyed white.

Right: The use of white fabric draped from the canopy of the bed gives the room a dreamy, ethereal air. This is heightened by interesting patterns of light and shadow created by the positioning of the fabrics.

Above: Thanks to the color white, serenity is an easy effect to achieve. Doors, frames, windows, furniture, materials, and floors in this color create a relaxing atmosphere fit for a bedroom.

Right: A room whose floor, walls and ceiling are white will gain luminosity but lose depth. The color white causes the loss of reference points, so the bed seems to be right in the foreground.

To overcome the dead space usually found in a room with a sloping ceiling, an object can be placed in this corner, like the shelved headrest in the photograph. The alternative is to have a dark corner that is terribly difficult to decorate or furnish unless filled by an item made to measure. The part of the room behind the headrest can be used for storage.

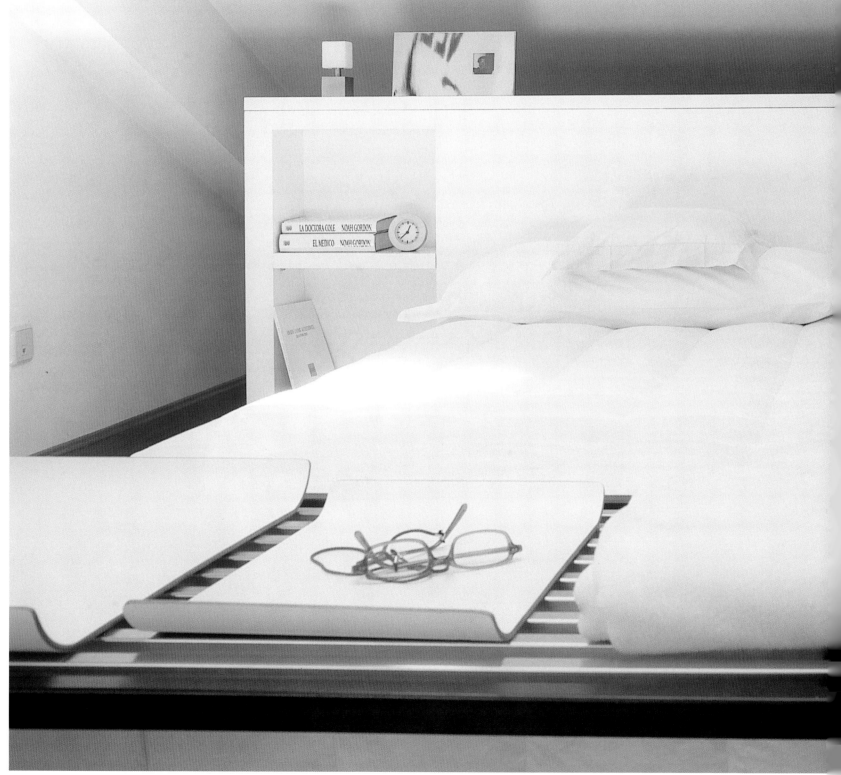

White, stripped furniture, typical in Nordic interiors, can also be a strong presence in Mediterranean environments. This color is also a safe bet for the linen in a home: a set of white sheets appears classically elegant.

Above: Although it can appear to be a color of just one tone, white possesses dozens of shades, ranging from pristine white to dirty white. Here, the meeting of two walls in two shades of this color mark the corner of a room.

Right: The flexibility of white, perhaps the least aggressive color in the entire spectrum, means it can be combined with decorative details that have strong character, such as the industrial style table lamp and the black leather cushion in this bedroom.

Left: White is synonymous with light, and reflects natural as well as artificial lighting very well. As well as being timeless, white light is generous, and guarantees an open, bright room.

Above: The light that falls on a bed should be indirect and diffused so as not to project shadows that disturb reading, for example. A white screen that diffuses the light is the best solution.

Left: The monochromatic style of the room is balanced by decorative elements that break up the harmony: in this case two metallic lamps of striking and fine lines and a small table positioned next to each one. The Ray and Charles Eames chair, the most valuable piece in the room, is thus converted into the *piece de resistance*.

Above: Lightness is another effect that this color can achieve: In this dressing room, for example, the rotund presence of these big wardrobes is minimized after being lacquered in a tone of white that, thanks to the artificial lighting, acquires several shades.

Above: Everyday objects, such as a pair of candlesticks, take on different dimensions when painted in white. This color plays the leading role in the bedroom on the right, where it matches the glass and the mirror and enhances the fantastic wooden floor.

Right: The spider lamp and bohemian-styled glass doors make a decisive contrast with the modern style of the rest of the bedroom furniture. The color white that dominates the room allows the effortless coexistence of both styles.

Above: Minimalism would not exist without white, perhaps the only color on which black, rather than becoming an uncomfortable element, is very aesthetic.

Right: The owner of this dwelling was obliged to install the toilet and bathroom cupboards in a corner of the bedroom. The white color of these "intrusive" pieces enables them to go relatively unnoticed.

White like wax, like ice, like snow, like paper... There are a thousand shades of this color, which is also attractive lightly stripped, as in the vault of the bedroom shown here.

To enhance a valuable decorative feature, like the painting in the photograph, it should be hung on a white wall and illuminated from the top by a spotlight that emits a strong, filtered, and lightly diffuse light. This results in the feature standing out in a completely neutral setting.

Left: The roughness of the engraved cement floor is balanced by the white color of the walls. This kind of floor may appear cold, although it is more resistant and very attractive from an aesthetic point of view thanks to its natural colors and primitive, yet elegant finish.

Above: With white background even the strangest color can be enhanced, such as the crimson of the gauze material placed on the bed or the faded red of the flooring of this bedroom.

White is a good way to hide an imperfection, although sometimes it is applied in a deliberately uncaring way to give more charm to a room, as is the case in this dressing room, whose floor has been painted with white brushstrokes.

A serene room, almost monastic, has been achieved here, where white plays the absolute leading role, especially in the textures and curtains.

In this case the most subtle decorative details are those that manage to breathe life into the room: the cushions and woollen blanket, the delicate Japanese-inspired pattern on the curtains, and the stressed wooden chair painted white.

Left: White is the most comfortable colour when decorating a house. Almost all objects and decorative details we could think of are available in white: from photo frames to trays, bedside tables, lamps and jugs.

Above: Although much more delicate than darkly colored furniture, white upholstery is a much safer option when acquiring a sofa or an armchair. Furthermore, this color gives extra light to a corner with little natural light.

The white flower is without doubt a classic, since it can adapt to any space and always appear elegant. In flowers, white also acquires dozens of shades. It is even tinged by green, as is the case with these lilies placed in glass vases on this small table.

Right: The different lights and the details of colour (such as the blue square on the bed's headrest or the sliding door in the bedroom) help to delimit the different volumes in a space decorated exclusively with white objects.

This bed, inspired from a traditional Japanese bedroom, integrates the white in its built-in headboard with shelving, in its inclined covering, which acts as a canopy and in the sheets, pillows and bedspread. The only concession towards another colour is the wooden frame and the stool at the foot of the bed.

Above: The serenity of white means that it is widely used in the decoration of children's bedrooms, where it can be combined with beige, pink, blue, or any other tone. White is a balancing color, providing equilibrium in moments of intensity.

Right: Canopy beds, especially if they are in a room with wooden floors and furniture, add a neo-romantic, fairy tale air to the room.

Above: The upholstery, the rugs, and the bed linen help to change the look of the furniture and of the rooms they adorn. A plain blanket, like the one here, brings personality to the bedroom.

Right: White is sympathetic to simple and elegant decorative details as well as to more baroque and daring features.

All colors combine with white, but this tone goes especially well with beige, which, like white, is a neutral, classic tone. The structure of this bed has been upholstered with a thick beige material that accentuates the effect of the white linen. A woollen rug is the other detail in beige.

Kitchens

In recent decades, the kitchen has gone from being the place where the servants worked or the housemaid kept herself hidden to becoming the heart of the home. Today, this room has become a common family meeting place and, in many cases, a substitute for the dining room. Its new functions make it central to the contemporary home, so its design is especially cared for. Being a clean, timeless colour, that enlarges the space and provides extra light, the option of a white kitchen is becoming more and more popular in homes—lacquered or white wooden furniture, marble or Corian worktops, white flooring and immaculate walls are all becoming more common. A series of accessories and materials, from lights to stools that look like crockery, round off the application of the ranges of white in the kitchen. All combine to create the perfect tone and simple, clean, and uncomplicated spaces.

The dining surfaces of today's kitchens, integrated into the workspace, have made it a substitute for the dining room. The refined, minimalist lines of the new kitchen furniture make this room, till now hidden in the house, a meeting point.

Above: The range of white accessories for the kitchen is extensive: from classic china sets to the most modern stools. White accessories do not clutter spaces and rarely go out of fashion.

Right: White is the color of cleanliness, thus its predominance in kitchens. In this case, the enormous kitchen work area is complemented with two designer stools from the sixties, also in white.

Left: If the kitchen is part of a larger space, its visual impact can be softened by choosing kitchen cupboards without handles. They will resemble wardrobes and help to reduce the aesthetic weight of the kitchen.

Above: White is a simple and clean color, that creates sober, and especially light spaces. Applied to cupboards it has the power to remove this furniture's visual weight, no matter how big they are, meaning the storage function does not overwhelm.

A white curtain can be a good way to filter the natural light that shines through a kitchen door or window. Where possible this should be positioned away from the kitchen burners or the oven, thus minimising any possible damage. Three cream-colored stools give the kitchen a livelier feel without breaking up the predominantly white ambience.

In this kitchen the majority of the objects and utensils are kept in view, contradicting the minimalist aesthetic. To balance this visual display, the color white has been chosen as a unifying element, with a spectacular fridge of retro design becoming the centerpiece. Fruits and flower vases strategically placed by the owners bring color to the space.

All the rooms in the house, from the bathroom to the kitchen, can be decorated in neutral and natural tones, but it is important to use the existing features in the room as a cornerstone of the decorative scheme.

Above: In this ultramodern kitchen white acts as a background to emphasize the metallic finish of some of the appliances, such as the two extractor fan hoods, or to emphasize the deep blue of a glass panel that divides the worktop into two areas.

Right: In this kitchen the emphasis has been on the crossing of horizontal straight lines and vertical lines. The result is a visually modern room of somber aesthetic where no one detail takes prominence away from another.

Left: White is the ideal color for those who wish to give their kitchen a futuristic, science fiction-inspired air. In this case the light filtering through the blinds on the back wall creates a relaxed and tranquil atmosphere. Not even the white wooden floors break this Zen harmony.

Above: Combining white surfaces with other light wooden ones in kitchens is a featured imported from the Nordic countries, and is becoming more and more popular in interior design. The different honey tones of the wood harmonize well with the neutral white.

In this case, the spaces of the kitchen and dining room have been divided by the contrast of the color white (for the kitchen, the marble and cupboards) against the jet black color of the chairs around the glass table. To balance the contrast, some white curtains have been chosen in order to unify the room.

White is a color of a thousand shades, with a potential to create attractive and timeless spaces. This kitchen, decorated almost entirely in white, becomes a very evocative room thanks to the use of this color.

The simplicity of minimalist interiors requires the application of white, since this color has the power to make other colors (like the orange of this chair) stand out as well as other shapes and textures.

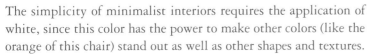

On these two pages are two completely different styles of kitchen in which the use of white coincides. The kitchen, is based on minimalist designs, whereas the one above is much more baroque in style and is built around a striking piece of furniture: a low cupboard on which all types of decorative items have been placed. A curtain of transparent round panels separates the two elements in a discreet manner (the kitchen space and the one dominated by the cupboard.)

155

Bathrooms

There is perhaps nothing more pleasurable than stepping into a bath or a shower in a completely white bathroom, flooded in light, then wrapping up in a bathrobe or a freshly ironed towel of the same color. Symbolizing purity and cleanliness, white is a classic in this room of the house, perhaps the most private of all. Marble, porcelain, and white textiles have always had an important presence in bathrooms. Today they are combined with natural woods, glass, metal, and perhaps a speck of color, but the presence of white continues to dominate these spaces. The white color lends a significant importance to other decorative color features (some flowers, a plant, the wood of the cupboard, or a brightly colored towel).

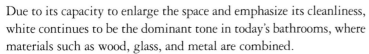

Due to its capacity to enlarge the space and emphasize its cleanliness, white continues to be the dominant tone in today's bathrooms, where materials such as wood, glass, and metal are combined.

Designers have put special emphasis on bathroom furniture and accessories, which match the transparencies, the materials, and the white backgrounds. Today's bathroom furniture is so well cared for from an aesthetic point of view that it can be integrated into a bedroom without any problem as in the case above.

White is especially recommended for those bathrooms that do not benefit from a natural source of light. A large mirror, like the one in the photograph above, allows for the optimal use of the little light it does receive. In these cases, leaving the walls bare and going for similarly colored decorative features is also a good idea.

Having a generously sized bathroom solves numerous problems and makes for an interesting and flexible use of all the features in the room. In this case, the owners have included a bathtub, from where views through the window can be enjoyed at leisure. Another factor helping to increase space is the absence of any items on the floor, (except of course the bathtub).

A white background accentuates the theatrical effect that a velvet curtain provides in this small toilet. The sum of all the colors of the spectrum, white boasts hundreds of tones, from that of a bar of handsoap to that of porcelain.

In this case the toilet has been concealed behind a medium high marble wall. The bathtub and shower are in line, and the use of a transparent screen for the shower, instead of reducing the area, visually amplifies the available space. This is really an obligatory solution in small bathrooms or in those that rely on artificial lighting.

Changing natural light shows the shades of white, which is a color
that acquires a host of tones and makes textures, such as the cotton
of the towels, stand out especially well.

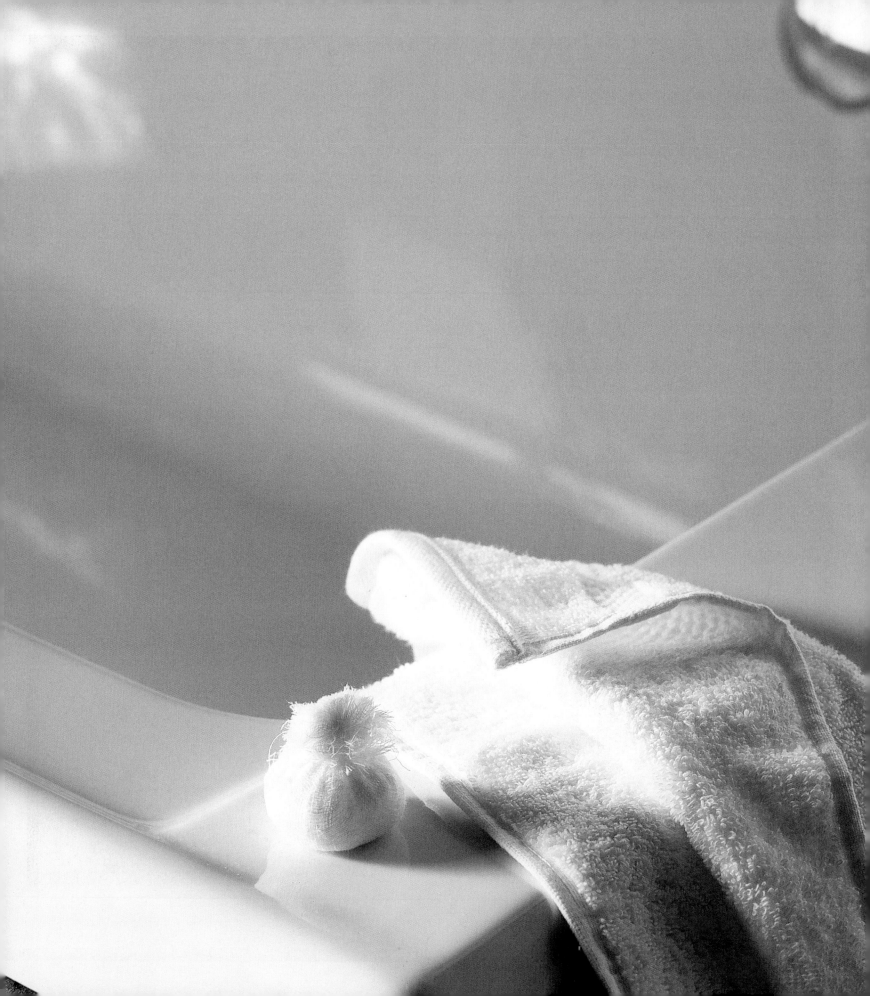

Above: White combined with glass is practically synonymous with modernity. The transparency of glass combined with the subtlety of white provides any room with lightness, an effect that the mirrors are there to reflect.

Right: Today the bathroom is a world away from its old conception as purely a wash area. Nowadays, a bathroom is also a space for relaxation and the well-being of body and mind. White marble, large mirrors, and white towels are, in this case, synonymous with comfort.